LOVING ON PURPOSE

PARENTING SERIES

Loving Our Kids
ON PURPOSE
PREPARING OUR KIDS FOR THE KINGDOM OF GOD

WORKBOOK

DANNY SILK

www.lovingonpurpose.com

This manual has been designed
to be used in conjunction with the associated
DVD series *Loving Our Kids On Purpose*

Second Edition © copyright 2012 Danny & Sheri Silk
www.LovingOnPurpose.com

Cover Graphics by Linda Lee
Interior Design and Formatting by Lorraine Box
Developed by Laurie Freeman
Outlined by Katie McIntyre

ISBN: 978-0-9833895-8-3

To my life partner Sheri,
to my children and grandchildren

I pray that our ceiling is your floor
of love, honor and faith.

Laurie Freeman

thank you for your love and support
in making this project successful

CONTENTS

"It is very difficult to promote Danny Silk's ministry without sounding like I have the need to exaggerate. But the truth is, in the circles I run in, he is without equal. His discernment gives him access to root issues that have become obstacles to relational peace and blessing, while his wisdom enables him to be a 'builder of families' and an 'architect of relationships.' I heartily recommend Danny and all his materials to help bring about God's best for your life."

Bill Johnson
Senior Leader Bethel Church

If you are a parent, this series is for you. This workbook has solutions to many of your everyday questions. Although there isn't a formula for raising mistake-free children, there is hope that you can learn to control yourself, no matter what choices or lessons your children invite into their lives. The peace and power that comes from making the right adjustments, in the presence of your child's mistake, is phenomenal. If you complete this material, you are going to see tremendous breakthrough in both your own personal peace and in the loving connections you can form with your child.

We want to propose to you that freedom is a top priority in Heaven because it is what makes loving relationships possible. Heaven's culture of relationships is vastly different than most everything we see on earth because God, the Father, is less interested in compliance and much more interested in love. For this reason, He is trying to prepare us to live absolutely free lives, in an environment of unlimited options, more than trying to keep us from sin. We would like to show you how to love your own kids with this goal in mind. This is the heart of Loving our Kids on Purpose.

Danny & Sheri

Introduction

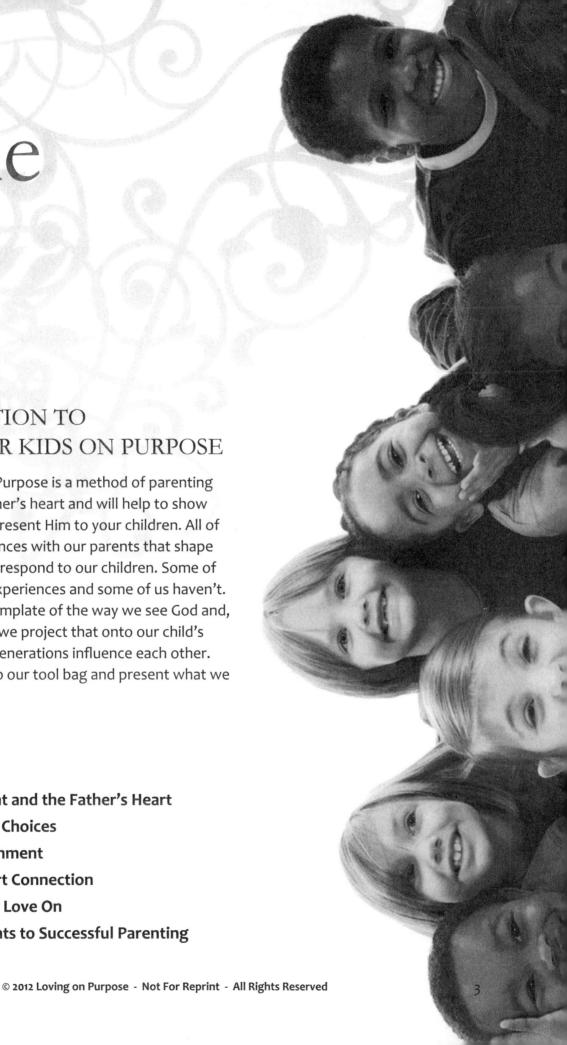

session

one

INTRODUCTION TO LOVING OUR KIDS ON PURPOSE

Loving Our Kids on Purpose is a method of parenting that reveals the Father's heart and will help to show you how to best represent Him to your children. All of us have had experiences with our parents that shape the way we see and respond to our children. Some of us have had great experiences and some of us haven't. We have a built in template of the way we see God and, without realizing it, we project that onto our child's template. It's how generations influence each other. We simply reach into our tool bag and present what we have to our kids.

SESSION TOPICS

Introduction

New Covenant and the Father's Heart

Freedom and Choices

Fear of Punishment

Heart-to-Heart Connection

Keeping Your Love On

Key Ingredients to Successful Parenting

INTRODUCTION

- Your parenting style is based on the way you perceive your experiences and the template that you were given.

- When you try to be powerful in your own home and hit resistance, you usually reach into your tool bag and pull out what your parents have given you.

- If you don't intentionally replace what you were given as a small child, then it's downloaded as your normal, your template.

- Your perception of love, authority, respect, obedience, the goals of parenting and the practice of relationship are transferred to you before you have had time to understand it.

"You're the best parent your child could have.
No one loves them like you do!"

~ Sheri

What parenting tools do you have in your tool bag that have been passed on to you?

Which tools are you currently using? How are they working for you?

....

....

....

....

....

....

NEW COVENANT AND THE FATHER'S HEART

Isaiah 59:21 The Message   *"'As for me,' GOD says, 'this is my covenant with them: My Spirit that I've placed upon you and the words that I've given you to speak, they're not going to leave your mouths nor the mouths of your children nor the mouths of your grandchildren. You will keep repeating these words and won't ever stop.' GOD'S orders."*

- The heart of the Father is that we build lasting relationships from generation to generation. There is a momentum in how we train our children.

- We create a culture that our children will instill in their life and pass on to their children.

- We want to lay a solid foundation where God's covenant can be laid and where our children can say, "I understand the difference between fear and love, freedom and control."

> If I give my children freedom, respect & honor in my home, they'll download a culture that makes every other culture pale in comparison.

Jeremiah 31:31-32 NKJV   *"Behold, the days are coming, says the LORD, when I will make a new covenant with the house of Israel and with the house of Judah-not according to the covenant that I made with their fathers in the day that I took them by the hand to lead them out of the land of Egypt..."*

- The new covenant transition is where we move from an external to an internal relationship with God.

- No longer is there some kind of force on the outside that's trying to control me. Now there is an internal force that I relate to from the inside out.

- An external control system says, "I make decisions based on: Who's going to be mad at me? Who's going to punish me if I cross the line or if I do something wrong?"

- An internal control system says, "I make decisions based on: How's that going to work out for me? I have choices to make and a quality of life that I'm responsible to cultivate. What am I going to do with this opportunity?"

List the values and characteristics that you want to cultivate in your home.

Take some time and ask the Lord what He is saying about the destiny over your child/ren and make a list of prophetic words they have been given.

....

....

....

....

....

FREEDOM AND CHOICES

Genesis 2:9 NKJV *"And out of the ground the LORD God made every tree grow that is pleasant to the sight and good for food. The tree of life was also in the midst of the garden and the tree of the knowledge of good and evil."*

- Freedom is important to God.

- You can't have love if you don't have freedom; you can't have freedom if you don't have a choice.

> **"How do I create a free place for my children where they have a choice?"**

- My job is not to teach my children to let me control them; my job is to teach my children to control and manage themselves, no matter what's going on in the world around them.

- The role of the Holy Spirit is to teach us to manage ourselves in all the freedom that God has afforded us.

6

Are there any areas in your parenting where you find yourself fighting for control?

List what they are and ask yourself how you can respond in a different way.

....

....

....

....

....

FEAR OF PUNISHMENT

2 Timothy 1:7 NKJV   *"For God has not given us a spirit of fear, but of power and of love and of a sound mind."*

- Do I want to put my child on a track where they make decisions based on the fear of punishment or where they realize there are relational consequences for their poor choices?

1 John 4:18 NIV   *"There is no fear in love. But perfect love drives out fear, because fear has to do with punishment. The one who fears is not made perfect in love."*

- The goal of the culture of Heaven is for us to experience maturing love.

- If my goal is love and freedom, I need completely different tools than if my goal is control and intimidation.

- "I have all the power and you have no power," is not true; it's painful when parents discover this.

yellow truck, red truck

How do you create a free place where your children have choices and decisions to make?

....

....

....

....

....

....

HEART-TO-HEART CONNECTION

Psalms 32:8 NKJV *"I will instruct you and teach you in the way you should go; I will guide you with My eye."*

The new covenant is about the power of relationship and love, not about behavior and obedience. Behavior and obedience happen, but they happen as a by-product of the ultimate, which is a heart-to-heart connection. It is the ability to lead someone with love.

- It's not about being controlled; it's about being affected, influenced, and connected.

- If I look into your eyes, I see your heart. If I see your heart, then I see how my behavior and my choices are affecting you. Then, I have a decision to make.

- Am I going to adjust how my behavior, seeing how it's affecting you? This is the test of love, of covenant, and of relationship.

Are you adjusting your behavior based on how you see it is affecting your children? If so, how?

....

....

....

....

....

....

....

....

KEEPING YOUR LOVE ON

Psalms 32:9 NKJV   *"Do not be like the horse or like the mule, Which have no understanding, Which must be harnessed with bit and bridle, else they will not come near you. "*

- I need to manage me no matter what you do today. My love is going to stay on towards you. No one controls my love but me.

- These little people just keep being people, their whole life. They're people, there's nothing you can do about it, so just get good at keeping your love on.

  > I don't want you to have to be governed by pain; I want you to be governed by love.

- Your children can learn to make adjustments to protect your connection or they can learn how to survive the relationship with you.

- If your child is making decisions based on whether or not they are going to be punished or hurt, they are not being obedient; they are preserving themselves in relationship with you.

- The foundation is to preserve the heart-to-heart connection; teach them what you need, and give them access to your heart.

- Parents, especially of teenagers, pretend that they don't have an emotional response to their child's craziness. Show them your heart. Let them feel the weight of who you are in this relationship. Let them feel the responsibility.

> **Teach your children the strength of love and heart-to-heart connection.**

John 14:15 NASB *"If you love Me, you will keep My commandments."*

- Jesus died so that we would be free. It's a brand new way of relating; it's rooted and grounded in love, not in the fear of punishment.

Can I Go To Public School?

When our son Levi was 14 years old, he was going to a Christian school. He said, "Mom and Dad, I want to go to public high school." He had 12 classmates at Bethel Christian School in the 8th grade and wanted to go to a school with 1,800 students? Let's do the math real quick. How many poor choices are there at a school with 1,800 students? All of them…Dang! There are a lot of poor choices there. "Ok. Um. Son, we're scared. We're so scared. Look at your mom. Look at how scared your mom is! Honey, why would we be geniuses to ever say yes to that idea?"

"Why would you be geniuses? Because, I will not break your heart."

Hmm, I wasn't expecting that. "That's a pretty good answer Son." He understood something. It was his job to manage his half of us and that he would not use the freedom that he'd been given to injure our relationship. He would manage himself.

For four years of high school, that's exactly what he did. He managed himself. He used that freedom as life for him, knowing that there were lots of choices and options that would injure our relationship, but he chose to protect our connection.

How would you have handled this situation as a parent?

What tools or techniques can you use from this story for your own family?

....

....

....

....

....

....

"You're the best parent your child could have.
No one loves them like you do!"

~ Sheri

KEY INGREDIENTS TO SUCCESSFUL PARENTING

1. **CONNECTION:** Heart-to-Heart

2. **EMPOWERMENT:** "What are you going to do?"

3. **SAFE PLACE:** "I can handle your mistakes."

4. **UNCONDITIONAL LOVE:** "Nothing can separate you from my love."

The key for successful parenting is to protect the heart-to-heart connection with your child. It helps to give your children power in relationship so they can practice their responsibility. It creates a safe place for them to convey the message, "I can handle who you are as a human being. I can deal with people. I can handle your mistakes. There is nothing you could ever do to threaten my love for you. My love for you is absolutely unconditional."

Discuss these questions together as a class or in small groups.

1. What stood out to you the most in this introductory session?

2. How were you raised? What was the model of parenting used in your home?

3. Was the parenting you received based on fear of punishment or freedom? What did that look like? Give an example.

4. Discuss what you want to see in your own parenting as a result of this class.

Take some time this week to answer the questions below and apply the concepts you've learned in this session.

1. Think of a situation that happened this past week where you found yourself responding like your own parent would have. Describe.

2. In your own life, do you find yourself being controlled by an external control system or an internal control system? Explain.

3. On a scale of 1-10, how is your heart-to-heart connection with your child? How do you plan on building a greater connection?

4. Go through this session and write down the answers to the REFLECT questions in your workbook.

session

two

Language of Empowerment

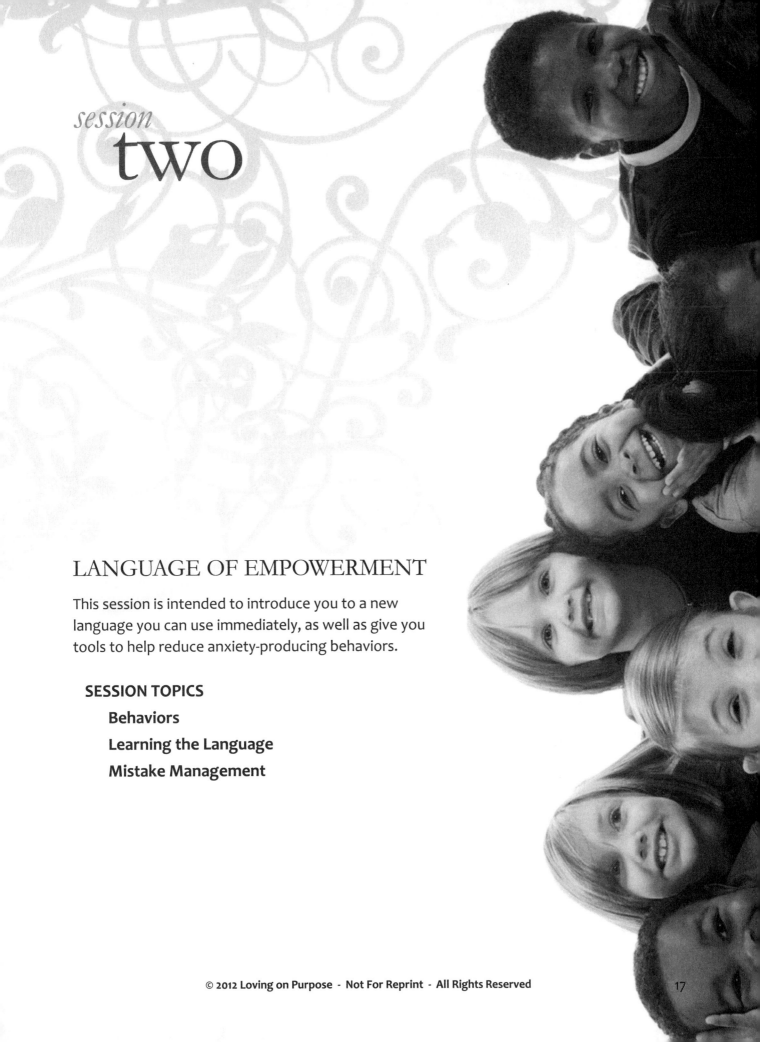

session
two

LANGUAGE OF EMPOWERMENT

This session is intended to introduce you to a new language you can use immediately, as well as give you tools to help reduce anxiety-producing behaviors.

SESSION TOPICS
Behaviors
Learning the Language
Mistake Management

BEHAVIORS

The following list is generated from parents all over the world when asked this question: What behaviors or tasks your children complain about would you like to see eradicated from your home?

Behavior List

Disrespect	Defiance	Hitting/Bullying
Chores	Back talk	Low self esteem
Homework	Lying	

- We want to reduce the anxiety producing behaviors while they're learning.

- When we try to control these behaviors in our children, we soon find that we've lost control of ourselves.

- The trap is the belief that we can control others.

- How are you going to manage yourself, no matter what your children do?

- Learn to successfully keep your child's problem their problem.

What are the three main behaviors you want to see removed from your home? What plan do you have to remove them?

....

....

....

....

....

LEARNING THE LANGUAGE

One-Liners[1] *The following phrases/tools originated by Love and Logic®*

I know

Probably so

That could be

I don't know

Nice try

- These sayings are a way of keeping your sanity, while your children are losing theirs.

- These one-liners will help you stay away from entering into an argument or power struggle.

- Never argue with children.

- The goal is to reduce and remove the anxiety-producing behaviors that children present to us while they are learning; it is not to control them or their thinking.

- Have a plan in your approach to them learning, or their learning is going to catch you off guard.

Example:

Child: *It's not fair.*

Parent: *I know.*

Child: *You know it is not fair.*

Parent: *Probably so.*

Child: *You can't say I know, when it is not fair.*

Parent: *I know.*

Child: *You are mocking me.*

Parent: *I am not trying to honey. I love you.*

---

[1] Love and Logic ® (see further information regarding this in *References & Resources*)

"The best way I stay in control of me is by using the one-liners. They are a lifesaver! I'm able to teach my child that I value us by not engaging in the disrespect battle that so many parents get sucked into."

~Brittney

- Be sure to convey the message, "I love you," while they are learning to manage themselves.

- Make a decision not to argue with your children.

- It's important not to assault a connection with an argument.

- Your job is to manage you and not to control the way they think, what they feel, or whether they approve of your judgment.

- Maintain a heart-to-heart connection.

- You will be able to have influence and give input, if you have a connection.

Oh No!

"I'm sad for you. I know this is going to hurt some. You are a smart kid. You will probably learn something helpful through this situation. I love you very much."

- This is a response to their big mistakes.

- It is simply to communicate "I am sad for you" to your child.

- There is a lesson coming that is going to carry a lot of consequences. It is probably not going to be fun, but you are going to love them through the process.

What are you going to do?

"You have the power to do something about your problem. I am sure that you will find a great solution to this issue in your life. If you need my help, I am here to help you. I love you very much."

- This response is giving them power for their own decisions.

- How is that going to work out for you? (This helps the child realize it's their problem.)

- You want to help a person who has a problem. You don't have a solution for anyone who does not have a problem.

- When you say, "What are you going to do?" And they say, "I don't know." Now you can take your pearls of wisdom and throw them into the conversation. You are talking to someone with a problem.

- Your child will be learning lessons about the consequences of their decisions.

- You will be the one who comes along side and helps bring out the best in them because they are actually taking responsibility for a mess they made and are cleaning it up.

No Problem

"No problem for me ... possible problem coming up for you! I love you very much."

- Have a plan. Know what you are going to do with you.

- Don't be afraid of your child's response, disobedience, or opposition.

- Have a smile on your face because you are not the one with the problem.

- Parents can be so dependent on their child's obedience, that when the child feels powerless and wants to feel powerful (I am not budging), the parents don't know what to do.

Fun-to-be-with

"I need you to learn what I need in this relationship. I will love you while you learn this valuable lesson."

- This is a requirement or experience between you and me.

- I need you to be fun to be with.

- Set limits with your child.

- Teach them to respect and value what you need from them in the relationship.

- In order to protect and build a connection, there have to be two powerful people in this relationship.

If I teach you that there is only one person in this relationship, you will have no respect for what I need. I am hurt and offended. I have trained you to disregard me in this relationship.

How effective are you in teaching your children to value and respect what you need in your relationship with them?

By incorporating this new language, and not arguing with your child, how will it improve your relationship and the environment in your home?

Why is it important for children to be able to learn the consequences of their own decisions?

....

....

....

....

....

MISTAKE MANAGEMENT

Britt's Lunch

When Brittney was about nine years old, Sheri decided she was no longer making lunches. She bought the groceries for lunches and put them in the cupboard. Brittney was all excited the first day. (This was intended to teach her to handle some of her responsibilities for her life. She was graduating to more responsibilities.) I (Danny) drove her to school. When I got home, guess what was on the counter? Her lunch. I looked at Sheri and she said, "She's going to call." (Phone rings.) Sheri looked at me and said, "Here we go!"

Britt: Hi mom, I forgot my lunch box on the counter.

Sheri: Oh the purple one?

Britt: Yes.

Sheri: Oh, there it is. I see it.

Britt: Mom, can you bring me my lunch?

Sheri: Sweetie, I am not going to the school today. (We live three blocks from the school.)

Britt: Oh, mom! That's not fair!

Sheri: I know.

Britt: Mom, please bring my lunch.

Sheri: I'm sorry Britt. I'm not going to the school today. What are you going to do?

Britt: I was going to call you and have you bring it.

Sheri: I know. I have an idea, if you would like to hear it.

Britt: What? (Sounding upset)

Sheri: Well, some kids wait around till after lunch and stay around the trash bin to see what they can find.

Britt: Ah, that's a stupid idea. I am not going to dig in the trash.

Sheri: I do have one more idea for you.

Britt: Is it any better than the last one?

Sheri: Maybe so. You could ask one of your friends if they want to share their lunch with you.

Britt: Oh, I don't want to ask anybody. I want my lunch. Can you please bring me my lunch?

Sheri: I am sorry. I am not going to school today. I have one more idea, though. You can go to the secretary and ask what happens when kids forget their lunch.

Britt: I don't want to talk to her. I am scared of her.

Sheri: Ok, that is all the ideas I have. I know you are going to figure this out. I love you very much. Good-bye. (Click.)

This is very hard to do. It is hard to let kids have their own problem. It is much easier to solve it for them… in this case to pull up at the school, walk in and say, "This is the last time. Don't think I will drive down here tomorrow! You have to take responsibility." It is way easier to do that.

So Brittney came home from school and she slammed the door. Sheri was thinking, "She hates me. Poor child." Then Brittney came in.

Sheri: What did you do?
Britt: Huh?
Sheri: What did you do for lunch today?
Britt: Oh, I shared lunch with Olivia.

Oh my goodness, she has a brain and it works at school!

- What you are going to do with you while your children are learning about them?

- Children don't want to be controlled, so they will fight for their freedom.

> I am going to manage myself while I teach you to manage you.

- You want to avoid a power struggle that goes back and forth for control.

- It's not a parent's job to control their child; it's to teach them to control themsleves and to be an example of what self-control looks like.

- They are going to make mistakes along the way and so will you.

- You are raising responsible, powerful children when you teach them to manage themselves.

"Every time I find myself in a power struggle with one of my children, as soon as I give them a choice, we both feel powerful again."

~ Ben

How do you respond when your child makes a mistake?

Are you allowing your children to live their life in front of you while learning through making mistakes? How?

How will you help them learn to be responsible for their own choices and decisions?

....

....

....

....

....

....

....

....

....

....

....

....

....

....

....

....

....

....

....

....

Discuss these questions together as a class or in small groups.

1. Think of situation where your child has made a mistake or failed to be responsible. What was your response? How will you respond differently with the tools you just learned?

2. Is it difficult for you to allow your child to come up with their own solutions to their problems? Explain.

3. What do you want your child to learn through the consequences of their own decisions? How will you help them with this?

Take some time this week to answer the questions below and apply the concepts you've learned in this session.

1. Use the new language of one-liners to respond to your child this week. Write down how it worked for you and the changes you see.

2. Danny teaches that a healthy relationship is two powerful people respecting each other. Does your relationship with your child reflect this? If so, what does it look like? If not, what can you do to create this kind of relationship?

3. Go through this session and write down the answers to the REFLECT questions in your workbook.

No Fear In Love

session
three

NO FEAR IN LOVE

This session is about the battle between fear and love and the environment you are creating in your home.

SESSION TOPICS

Intimidation and Fear

The Great Lie

Choices and Freedom

Successful Parenting

INTIMIDATION AND FEAR

Amygdala — An almond-shaped neuro structure involved in producing and responding to non-verbal signs of anger, avoidance, defensiveness, and fear

A small mass of gray matter that inspires aversive cues, such as the freeze reaction, sweaty palms, and the tense-mouth display

The amygdala also prompts release of adrenaline and other hormones into the blood stream, thus stepping-up an avoider's response and disrupting the control of rational thought.

- ° When you are frightened, your amygdala gets triggered because of something that happens in your environment; then you begin to guard and protect yourself.

- ° There is a disconnect that happens when you get scared and you begin to think more about yourself than anything else.

- ° Creating a situation for your child to have to fight back under your leadership and authority is not the way heaven works.

1 John 4:18 NIV *"There is no fear in love. But perfect love drives out fear, because fear has to do with punishment. The one who fears is not made perfect in love."*

- ° Fear and intimidation might work, but it is not the way heaven works.

- ° Fear has to do with punishment, but perfect maturing love casts out all fear.

Describe a time when you were frightened and your amygdala was triggered. How did you respond?

Are you creating an environment of fear and intimidation or love and freedom? Explain.

....

....

....

....

....

THE GREAT LIE

What do we believe to be true?

Violence = Power

Anger = Power

Other people control me

I can control other people

° Most people believe that they can get their way by introducing pain and suffering into the relationship.

° Adults don't know what to do with the word 'no,' so they think it's their job to teach children to give them control or they will inflict pain.

° As long as this lie is in operation in your relationship, you will feel powerless and will try to control the other person.

> The great lie...
> believing other
> people can control
> me and I
> can control
> other people.

° As soon as you stop believing, "I can control people," you will stop trying to control.

° It's your job to do something; it's not your job to get others to do something.

° I manage me and you manage you.

° Love is not about control… it is about freedom.

° Shared control is when we have an understanding that I am free and you are free.

° The only way to be free is to have a choice.

"Most of us have been raised believing the lies about power. The more I believe you control you and I control me, the more we get to experience the exchange of love and life without the stuff that gets in the way."

~Ben

Is "the great lie" showing up in your parenting? If so, how?

What happens when you don't get your way in relation-ships? What tactics do you use to try to get others to do what you want? (Example: get angry, aggressive, mopey, pouty, weepy, sweet, etc.)

What truth do you want to replace instead of the lie?

....

....

....

....

CHOICES AND FREEDOM

Why Choices?

Control...one of the deepest needs within humans. If you threaten control you trigger a "panic response" in people and children are people.

> Your goal as a parent is to create a safe place where love can rule and fear can be extinguished.

○ God does not parent you through control, intimidation and punishment.

○ God parents you through unconditional love and trusting you with freedom.

○ When people aren't given choices, we are creating the worst in them.

○ When you take somebody's choice away and try to rule over them, they disconnect and begin to protect themselves.

Levi and Taylor's Bed Time

I remember when Levi and Taylor were four and six years old and we were ready to introduce freedom at bedtime. So, they got a choice. "Hey guys! It's *room time*[1]! I don't want to see you and don't want to hear you until morning. Good night." Taylor couldn't believe it. "Can we leave the light on?" "Don't want to hear you, don't want to see you till morning." "Can we read a book?" He's four he can't read a book. "Don't want to hear you, don't want to see you till morning." "Can we play with our toys?" "Don't want to hear you, don't want to see you till morning." He looks at Levi. Quick, let's go to bed before they come to their senses... and off they go.

Now, this is like putting two Labrador puppies in a box and telling them not to touch each other. Off they go to their room. Do I think they're going to fail? Of course they are! They're four and six. They're in the height of their mistake-making career. So pretty soon I hear, "Hee hee, ha ha, thump, thump, thump." So, I open the door and say, "Hey guys! Are you tired or do you need something to do?" "We're not tired! I'm not tired." "Are you tired? I'm not tired." I say, "Come here," and I lead them down the hallway. I open the garage door and say, "Levi, here you go. Here's a broom. Put the dirt in a pile and when you get done, put the

---

[1] *Room time*, Love and Logic ®

pile in the bucket over there. Ok? If you're tired, you can go to bed, but if you're not tired, I have something else for you to do." I shut the door.

I take Taylor out to the back patio and there is a piece of cement about four feet by six feet. It's got like eight leaves on it. He's four years old and hasn't done a lick of work in his whole life. I say, "Son, sweep these leaves off. If you're tired when you're done, you can go to bed. If you're not tired, I have something else for you to do." "Ahhhh… ahhhh!" He sounds like somebody is skinning him. He's sitting there just crying and crying and crying.

Levi gets done. I say, "Hey buddy alright. Are you tired or do you need something else to do?" "I'm tired." "Alright buddy. (smooch) Goodnight."

Taylor is crying… he hasn't moved a leaf. I open the door and say, "Taylor, are you cold?" "Yeahhhhh!" "Here's your jacket." (Crying and crying.) "Hey, as soon as you're done, if you're tired, you can go to bed." He just drags it out however long and more crying. "Taylor, are you tired or do you want something else to do?" "T-t-t-tired." "Ok baby. All right. (Smooch!) Goodnight." And off he goes.

The next time… "Ok guys. It's room time! I don't want to hear you, don't want to see you until morning." They look at each other and off they go. Can you feel the weight of responsibility? Can you feel it? They are probably wondering if they can handle this kind of freedom. They are used to us yelling at them and telling them what to do and to get to sleep. They aren't used to being given freedom and choosing what to do. This was our bedtime routine for years and years.

Choice Samples:

Are you tired, or do you need something to do?

Feel free to join us for dinner when you've finished your chore. Take your time.

° Empowering children to make decisions, when they are little, is self-control practice.

° Offering choices and giving power is what begins to build responsibility.

° God empowers us beyond our wildest imagination.

° You want your child to feel empowered so they know what to do when freedom is offered to them.

Examples of choices parents can provide:

Do you want to go to bed now or when the TV show is over?

Do you want a piggyback ride or do you want to walk to bed?

Do you want to go potty first or brush your teeth first?

Do you want the red cup or the blue cup?

Do you want a story or no story?

Do you want to take a shower or a bath?

Do you want to wear this outfit or that outfit?

Do you currently give choices empowering your children to make decisions?

Can you think of additional ways to offer freedom by giving choices through everyday decisions?

....

....

....

....

....

....

....

....

SUCCESSFUL PARENTING

Three primary concepts

- ° Set firm limits

    Take good care of your self

    Tell others what you are going to do

    Use few words mixed with meaningful actions

- ° Give choices within limits

- ° Let the consequences mixed with empathy do the teaching

Set firm limits, knowing what you are going to do. Take good care of your self so you are better able to care for others. Learn how to protect the connection by lowering the anxiety. Trust that your kids will make mistakes; it's knowing what you're going to do with you when they do. Let the consequences of poor decisions be the master teacher. Your child will learn to understand the consequences of their decisions and when presented with a choice again they will make a great choice because they are geniuses.

"Give yourself a break!
Parenting can be the most emotionally draining experience if we compare ourselves
to other parents all the time."

~Sheri

Discuss these questions together as a class or in small groups.

1. What do you believe will make another person powerful?

2. How do you allow your children to be powerful?

3. In what areas of your parenting are you believing the great lie... other people can control me; I can control other people? How is this shown?

4. What situations bring the most anxiety in your home (where you feel out of control)? Discuss some ways the anxiety can be reduced.

Take some time this week to answer the questions below and apply the concepts you've learned in this session.

1. List areas of responsibilities where you can give your child more freedom with choices (ie. bedtime, homework, mealtimes, chores, etc.). Describe what that would look like.

2. Think of a recent situation where your child made a mistake and you came up with a solution to their problem. How could you have responded differently to help them come up with the solution to their own problem?

3. Go through this session and write down the answers to the REFLECT questions in your workbook.

session
four

Heart-to-Heart
Connections

session
four

HEART-TO-HEART CONNECTION

This session is about building your heart-to-heart connection with your children and keeping your love on.

SESSION TOPICS

Connection: The Goal of Relationship

The Best Kept Secret

Languages of Love[1]

    Gifts

    Touch

    Acts of Service

    Words of Affirmation

    Quality Time

Clean Up Your Messes

---

[1] The Five Love Languages (see further information regarding this in *References & Resources*)

CONNECTION   The Goal of Relationship

- We need a plan of how we are going to keep the love on.

- When we hit obstacles, we react and get filled up with anxiety.

- No matter what, we must keep our love on so the very best parent in us shows up.

What is the goal of your relationship?

A safe distance?

Or is the goal... a strong, loving connection

- To have a goal in any relationship is important, not just parenting.

- If you don't know what your goal is, you won't take responsibility for it.

What is the goal of your relationship?

A safe distance?

or is the goal ...

A strong loving connection?

- When somebody is scary or hurtful, we create a goal of a safe distance.

> If your goal is distance, you have decided to introduce anxiety into the relationship.

- You are the only one that can control your goal.

- Once you make your goal a strong loving connection, you immediately begin to reduce the anxiety between you and your child (or the other person).

- Always make preserving and strengthening your connection a priority.

- The worst thing to do while anxiety and fear are rushing into your relationship is to try and work out the problem while you are still disconnected.

- We need to get to a place of love and connection before working through a problem.

> *"I'm always looking for ways to build a heart-to-heart connection with my child so we have something to pull on when needed... Doing things that communicate love, the way they hear it."*
>
> ~ Ben

> When you find yourself in a disconnect with your child, step one is to get the connection back.

REFLECT

How does having a goal of connection in mind help your relationship?

....

....

....

....

....

....

THE BEST KEPT SECRET

Matthew 22:36-39 NIV *"Teacher, which is the greatest commandment in the Law?" Jesus replied, "'Love the LORD your God with all your heart and with all your soul and with all your mind.' This is the first and greatest commandment. And the second is like it: 'Love your neighbor as yourself.'"*

- Jesus makes the point that life is all about love.

- It's not about what you can do for me, your performance, your great behavior or about the rules you keep; it's about how good you get at managing your love towards other people.

- You are pouring your heart and soul into these little tiny people.

- Over and over you will get to demonstrate the greatest love of all... laying down your life for them.

John 15:13 NKJV   *"Greater love has no one than this, than to lay down one's life for his friend."*

- One of the ways we give our life for our children is to learn how they feel, "I love you."

What are some of the best-kept secrets in many families?

I love you very much

I value our relationship

Do you know how they hear "I love you"?

- For your child to experience their relationship with you as one of the most important relationships in your life, they need to feel and hear the message, "I love you very much."

- Even though it's not the way you hear "I love you," you need to demonstrate how they feel loved.

- Paying attention and understanding the love language of your child is important in keeping and restoring your connection.

- How they show love is usually how they hear love.

"Learn your child's love language."

~ Sheri

As you were growing up, did your parents have a difficult time showing love to you? How about to each other?

How are you at demonstrating "I love you," to your child? To others?

....

....

....

....

....

....

....

....

....

....

....

....

....

LANGUAGES OF LOVE

Adapted from Gary Chapman's book, *The Five Love Languages*

1. Gifts
2. Touch
3. Acts of Service
4. Words of Encouragement
5. Quality Time

GIFTS

Connection   *"You know me and were thinking about me when I wasn't even around!"*

- Gifts show that you were thinking about this person while you were away from each other.

- Gifts show that you know them and know how to affirm that about them.

- Gifts show that you remembered a special occasion, or any occasion, to express your love.

Disconnection   *"You don't care because you don't even know me or give me a passing thought."*

- Forget the gift

- Poor gift selection

- Miss a special occasion

The kiss of death is forgetting to bring a gift or bringing something that shows you don't really know them.

Do you experience love and connection through gifts?

Who in your family has this love language? What do they do to show this?

....

....

....

....

....

....

TOUCH

Connection   *"I feel connected when we are touching."*

- Physical contact

- Physical proximity

- Contact frequency

This is about feeling loved through affection. For example: you cannot sit on the couch by yourself without your child always wanting to be near you, lay on you, or want to be touched (like having their back scratched).

Disconnection   *"I feel rejected and neglected when you don't touch me."*

- Missed opportunities for touching

- Neglecting public displays of affection (PDA)

- Extended periods of time between touches

The kiss of death is not touching at all. If you are not a touchy person, you might not be trying to send the message of rejection, but that is the experience.

REFLECT

Do you experience love and connection through touch?

Who in your family has this love language? What do they do to show this?

....

....

....

....

....

....

ACTS OF SERVICE

Connection   *"I feel loved when you take care of things that are important to me."*

- Doing things for them

- Anticipating needs and meeting them

- Accomplishing specific tasks

Acts of service people like to be helped with what they need. They are taking note of the things that need to be done and feel loved and important when you help them.

Disconnection   *"You don't care about me, because you don't care about things that are important to me."*

- Neglect "help me" messages

- Angry responses to doing tasks

- Do tasks unrelated to request or need

The kiss of death is when your child thinks what's important to them isn't important to you. Help feels like love to them; not helping feels like invalidation or rejection.

Do you experience love and connection through acts of service?

Who in your family has this love language? What do they do to show this?

....

....

....

....

....

WORDS OF AFFIRMATION

Connection   *"I feel loved when I believe that you like me."*

- Words are life.

- Words contain value for who I am.

- Words say – "I believe in you!"

Life and death are in the power of the tongue. They are nourished by the idea that you like them, that you enjoy them. Smiling, laughing, and enjoying them is nourishment to their soul.

Disconnection   *"I feel rejected when your words are harsh."*

- Criticism slays them

- Super-sensitive to disapproval/correction

- Extended spans of time without value message.

Kiss of death is when you are angry or upset and you are trying to bring correction to your words of affirmation child through harsh words. They are sensitive to words and may need something like a hero sandwich.

Hero sandwich:

(Bread) I love you. You're amazing.

(Meat) That thing you're doing is not working for me at all.

(Bread) I love you. You're amazing.

When you say, "I love you," to a words of affirmation person, the words go in.
When you say, "I love you," to an acts of service person, they say pick up your socks.

Do you experience love and connection through words of encouragement?

Who in your family has this love language? What do they do to show this?

....

....

....

....

QUALITY TIME

Connection *"I feel loved when you show interest in me."*

- Sharing in an activity or conversation that is important to them

- Listening, being engaged in the conversation

- Willing participation

They will put their life on display and your job is to engage with them. It shows that you love them because you are interested in what interests them.

Disconnection *"I feel rejected when you don't value my interests."*

- Be distracted or uninterested

- Fail to listen well

- Fail to make time for connecting with them

Kiss of death is when you show... I don't have time and I'm not going to make time. When I'm with you, I'm distracted.

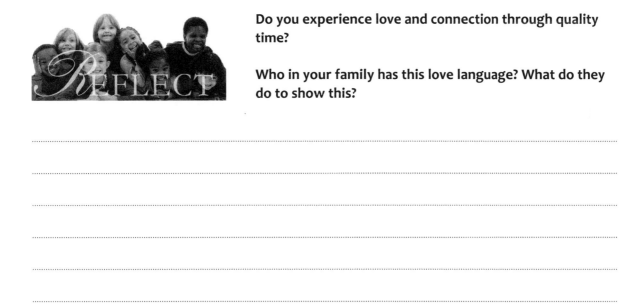

Do you experience love and connection through quality time?

Who in your family has this love language? What do they do to show this?

....

....

....

....

....

....

CLEAN UP YOUR MESSES

Connections occur through successful transfers of "I love you very much." Protect those connections. Keep connection your priority.

- When you have a disconnect, communicate you are sorry and that you didn't realize how it was affecting them.

- "I don't understand what you need from me, can you help me understand?"

- You have to get to the place where they feel they are receiving love.

Recall a time when you had to clean up a mess with your child and needed to apologize. What happened? How was your connection affected? How was the connection restored?

....

....

....

....

....

....

....

....

....

....

....

....

....

....

....

....

....

....

....

....

....

Discuss these questions together as a class or in small groups.

1. Why is it important to know each others' love languages?

2. Do you know your own love language? What is it? How do you know?

3. What are your spouse or child's top two love languages?

4. How good are you at communicating to them in their love language?

Take some time this week to answer the questions below and apply the concepts you've learned in this session.

1. Go to the website http://www.5lovelanguages.com and take the online assessment for yourself. Have your child take the online assessment for children.

2. List different ways you can love your children better through their language.

3. What are some ways you can keep your love on and keep the heart-to-heart connection with your child?

4. Go through this session and write down the answers to the REFLECT questions in your workbook.

55

Priority of Connection

THE PRIORITY OF CONNECTION

This session discusses the one thing we can give to this next generation... the skills to protect their connections. With all the options and freedoms our children have, we can give them the opportunity to tell themselves what to do and to prioritize their connections.

SESSION TOPICS

Protecting Connections

Fear and Control

Challenges

Staying Connected

Strength of Your Connection

PROTECTING CONNECTIONS

Relationship connections

Heavenly Father and Us

Husband and Wife

Parent to Child

Sibling to Sibling

Friend to Friend

- On a good day, I can control me.

- You want your children to grow into adults who knows how to tell themselves what to do and to prioritize their connections.

- The goal is to build connection with your child, protect that connection, nurture it and then maintain it.

Brittney Retells a Story of Being Missing for a Day

When I was 16 years old, we had just moved from Weaverville to Redding, and I was struggling with loneliness. I found myself in an Internet chat room with a boy who was returning some affection in a form that I had never known before. I had never had a boyfriend, so here I found myself chatting away with this boy and loving the attention. Late night phone calls turned into planning a time to meet. The week before we decided to meet, our family was in Los Angeles. I told my cousin what I was going to do so he was the only one who knew.

I told my mom that I was going to a party at a friend's house that day so I would have a reason to be gone all day. I then went and met this boy at a park. I ended up being gone for eight hours without any contact with my parents. My mom, at some point during the day, was trying to get a hold of me but she couldn't find me. She called the friend's house that I was supposed to be at and they told her, "Brittney never showed up." At that moment, what does any parent do? Their heart sinks into the pit of their stomach and every bad thought they could have is happening!

Through this process of trying to figure out where I was, she remembered my cousin and I had spent a lot of time together so he might know. He confessed and told her what I was doing… planning on meeting a boy I had met online at a park. He didn't know which one we decided to meet at and there are over 20 parks in Redding.

My mom was unable to get a hold of my dad because he was out of town and out of cell service. My mom was home alone and my dad and I had our only two cars. My mom was now spinning, "I don't know where my daughter is. What if something happens to her? I don't even know if she will be alive when I find her."

In the meantime, I was having a good old time. She called Kris and Kathy Vallotton, some of the only people we knew in town, and told them what was going on. Kris and Kathy prayed and the Lord ended up showing them exactly where I was, and they went right to me. There are a lot of parks in Redding and they drove right to me. I had been gone eight hours at that point. They found me in the dark, kissing some boy I had just met.

Kris talked to the boy and I called home, noticing I had over 40 missed calls. My dad answered and told me through his tears that he was just describing to the police what I looked like. In that moment, there was some pain of, "Oh gosh what did I just do?" But I couldn't go there because I was 16 years old and I knew it all so I was going to be mad instead. dI geared up for a fight.

While Kris and Kathy talked to my parents, I sat and waited for my punishment. I had my boxing gloves on and was ready to go. They came in the room and from my mom I could see anger, because being scared looks like anger. My dad was calm, but I was thinking he is probably in shock. So here we were, my mom and I were starting to butt heads, but my dad takes over and starts asking me questions like, "What were you doing? What were you thinking? What's going on? Why would you do this?"

I just spun in with, "You have no idea the pressure I have being your kid. I come down here and I'm Danny Silk's kid. Everyone knows everything about me. I'm constantly being compare to my friends. That's the pressure I live with being your kid and I hate it! I don't even know if I want to be a Christian anymore."

The response I got from my dad was crawling across the floor, putting his face and hands on my knees and saying, "Britt, I will give it up today. I will quit my job being a pastor. I will go back to being a social worker because my goal at the end of this is that you, your mom and your brothers are all on the other side. That's all I care about. If it's too much pressure for you, me being a pastor, I will stop today."

My dad emphasized the fact that his relationship with me was way more important than anything he could ever do for a living, more than where they lived, or what he did for a job. At that moment, I started to realize I was the most important thing and that I was the priority in their life.

Do your children know what your priorities are? How can you show them that they are a priority, like Danny's response to Britt?

How would you have responded in this circumstance?

....

....

....

....

....

FEAR AND CONTROL

- When your children are blinded by fear, loneliness, or pressure put on by themselves they lose a sense of who they are.

- You are not yourself when you are scared.

Anger...

- is fake power

- makes you feel powerful

- will push through boundaries

- will cause you to set limits instead of working through an issue

If you tend to be more of an aggressive personality or a verbal processor, ask yourself before responding in anger, "Am I going to want to clean up the mess I'm about to make with my words or can I be quiet and get my thoughts in order?"

"No problem is more important than your relationship with your child."

~ Sheri

Is responding in anger your 'normal?' How can you change that?

Can you think of a time when you spoke in anger and made a mess? How did you clean it up?

....

....

....

....

....

....

....

....

....

63

CHALLENGES

Challenge Points

Teen Loneliness/Peer Pressure

Punishing with Anger or Withdrawal

Personal Pressure or Outside Pressure

Overwhelming Fear

Freedom after Failure

- Your children are trying to be individuals in a world where it is difficult to be.

- Anxiety, fear and punishment will cause disconnection in relationship.

- The best time to work through an issue is when you're connected, not when you're disconnected.

- There are two main ways people punish; one is with anger and the other is to withdraw.

- Your child needs to know they are exactly who God created them to be and you don't want them to be anyone else.

> *"There is personal pressure that I put on myself being Danny Silk's daughter. Realistically, the pressure I took on as my own was a lie I chose to believe. I had a weak moment where I let someone else's words determine my life instead of believing who I am and what has always been reinforced through my parents and the Lord."*
>
> ~ Brittney

Freedom causes our personal responsibility to rise to the surface. We either rise with it or lose our freedom. The only way to cultivate freedom is through experiencing and learning how to handle an increasing number of options. Managing increasing options is how we expand our lives into ever-increasing abundance.

Do you see any of these challenge points in your child's life? How can you help them deal with them?

How do you affirm your children into being the individual God created them to be?

....

....

....

....

....

STAYING CONNECTED

- The best way to parent your child is… the way that works for your child and you.

- Nobody has perfect kids, not even God, and He's the BEST dad ever.

- When you are afraid and overwhelmed, you need to let somebody into your situation so they can help you and pray with you.

- It's okay to tell your friends when you're struggling.

> Love like you're going to get hurt. If you don't, your heart probably isn't completely open.

- Parents need to stick together.

- You can reconnect with your child by sharing your heart.

- There is freedom after failure.

"It's quite possible that this little person I brought into the world can hurt me more than anyone on the planet, but I'm going to love big."

~ Sheri

LOVING OUR KIDS
ON PURPOSE

Do you have other people in your life that you can be real with where you can share your struggles and fears? If not, how might this be beneficial?

How are you able to stay connected through the challenges?

What are some ways you have discovered that you need to parent your children differently? (ie. what works for one child doesn't work for another) Explain.

....

....

....

....

....

....

STRENGTH OF YOUR CONNECTION

What is the strength of your connection?

Your relationship with your child is like a bank account and the connection is what you have invested. When it comes time to make a withdrawal, can your relationship handle it? If you are going to make a withdrawal of $100 and you have only invested $5, you are going to be in the negative. Know that your connection and what you are depositing into your relationship is crucial.

> Love
> is better
> than rules.

- Your child needs to know they are worth the investment and that you are investing in them.

- Fill up your love account.

- Connection is the biggest priority.

66

- Your child should be able to look into your eyes, see love, and know how you feel about them.

- When your child is struggling or failing, you want to be right next to them or they won't receive what you have to give.

In the story of the prodigal son, this kid is making the worst mistake of his life. It's the only place in the Bible where you see a picture of a father running. Where do you want your father to be when you're failing? You want him right next to you.

> Rules without relationship equals rebellion.
>
> Bill Johnson

Psalms 32:8-9 NKJV   *"I will instruct you and teach you in the way you should go; I will guide you with My eye. Do not be like the horse or like the mule, which have no understanding, which must be harnessed with bit and bridle, else they will not come near you."*

How strong is your connection... as strong as a tissue or a leather strap?

What deposits have you made in your child?

Where is your love tank? Is the light on? Is the fuel low? How can you fill it up?

How are you going to work on strengthening your connection with your child?

....

....

....

....

....

....

....

Discuss these questions together as a class or in small groups.

1. What is your connection like with your child?

2. What are some ways you can strengthen that connection?

3. Are you allowing your children to make their own decisions? What is standing in the way?

4. How do you empower your child through freedom after they have failed?

Take some time this week to answer the questions below and apply the concepts you've learned in this session.

1. After evaluating your connection, how do you feel? Is there any area you need to improve?

2. Think about some situations where you put rules over your relationship. How can you express the priority of your connection?

3. List some successes in your connection with your child; with your spouse. Where have you felt totally connected? How did you feel?

4. Go through this session and write down the answers to the REFLECT questions in your workbook.

Loving Our Preschoolers On Purpose

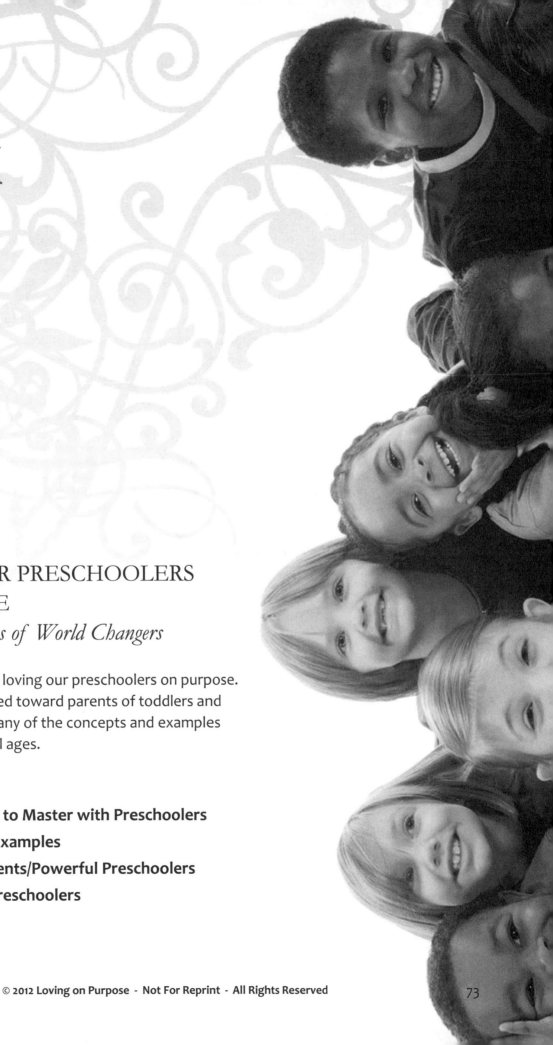

session •
six

LOVING OUR PRESCHOOLERS ON PURPOSE
Shaping the Lives of World Changers

This session is about loving our preschoolers on purpose. It is specifically geared toward parents of toddlers and preschoolers, but many of the concepts and examples can be adapted to all ages.

SESSION TOPICS

Primary Skills to Master with Preschoolers

Preschooler Examples

Powerful Parents/Powerful Preschoolers

Q and A for Preschoolers

PRIMARY SKILLS TO MASTER WITH PRESCHOOLERS

Build trust & a safe place

Teach self control

Create respect

Share control

Control you

Raising preschoolers is the truest test of being a parent. It's like a conspiracy and these little invaders have come with a chip in their body and they are designed to take over the planet. They are trying to figure out what's to be expected of them on this new planet and how to live in harmony with other earthlings. It's important for us as parents to build trust and create a safe place for these little people from our wrath, punishment and frustration.

We have to teach our preschoolers to control themselves because they think they are here to control us. If we don't pay attention, that is exactly what will happen. We will end up teaching them that they control our emotional life and our happiness.

We want our children to understand:

- They are powerful.

- They have choices to make.

- They are responsible for their choices at an early age.

- We have shared control.

- You control you and I control me.

Our job is to manage ourselves and to teach our children to manage themselves. There are two people in this relationship and a respect you require. We have to share the control back and forth with our children and remember that this is self-control practice for ourselves as well.

You giving your control, emotions, and the quality of your life to someone who still poops in their pants is a big mistake.

Preschooler Examples

Delani & The Toilet, as told by Britt

Taylor's Shorts in the Snow, as told by Danny

Fun or Room

Delani and the Toilet

My daughter, Delani, was about four years old and she was well informed of how potty training worked. One thing that she was having a hard time with was how much toilet paper should be applied. So we began teaching her, even down to the number of squares, because she was in preschool learning how to count. Here we were and she is more than capable of using the right amount of toilet paper. But this time around, for whatever reason, I noticed it became a game. She would put in huge amounts of toilet paper and it seemed to be whenever dad wasn't home. It was pure joy seeing how much of a reaction she could get out of me trying to plunge a whole roll of toilet paper down the toilet.

One day I went into the bathroom and saw this once again. My sweet angel had used almost a whole roll of toilet paper. I thought, "This is not fun for me. I am always cleaning up this mess." So I said, "Hey sweetie, what do you think about this toilet? Do you think it will flush or not flush?" She says, "Probably not flush." I said, "Right. So mommy has to go potty, and because I love you, I'm going to give you a choice. Would you like to clean it out before mommy goes potty or after mommy goes potty?" She looked at me like I was insane and says, "Ew!" "So before?" "YES!" "Ok sweetie, so what's going to happen is I'm going to need all that toilet paper taken out of the toilet. Would you like to do that with your bare hands or with a plastic bag over your hands?" Her jaw hits the floor. "What?" "By your bare hands or with a plastic bag?" Because she is a genius, she went with the plastic bag. So here she was fishing the toilet paper out of the toilet while crying and whining the whole time. She gets it out and the toilet ends up flushing fine. No plunger was required and I didn't end up cleaning a thing.

The next time she went into the bathroom longer than what was required I said, "What's going on in the bathroom?" She said, "Its okay mom, just in case you're wondering, I didn't use too much."

Watching my four-year old grasp the concept, this is "no fun for me" then having her experience the weight of her decision and live out the consequences at age four… that's powerful!

~ **Brittney**

What lessons do you think Delani learned from her experience cleaning out the toilet?

How do you think this will help her in the future? How can you apply this to a situation you are currently having at home?

....

....

....

....

....

Taylor's Shorts in the Snow

When our kids were little, we lived in a place called Mount Shasta. It was a unique experience for them when it snowed over night. There was a time when it snowed about two and a half feet in one night. Brittney was probably eight years old, Levi four and Taylor was around two. They ran to the front window and were in love with what they saw. It was beautiful! Two and a half feet of snow in one night is just beautiful. It's like wow! So Brittney wnt to her room and got her boots, her snow pants, her jacket, her gloves, and her hat. There she goes out the front door. Next came Levi with his boots, his snow pants, his jacket and his hat and out he went. Here comes Taylor. He had his boots, his jacket, his gloves and his shorts on and he headed out the front door. Sheri and I both wanted to stop him. We were thinking, "Oh my gosh! Oh my gosh! He's making a mistake! He's making a poor choice! This child is going to die if he goes out in the cold with his shorts on." We both looked at each other and out he went.

Britney and Levi were playing in the snow and they were all over the place. Taylor was standing on the front porch looking at it. We were at the front window looking out at the front porch watching and waiting. Pretty soon here he came back in and we met him at the front door. "Taylor, don't you want to go out and play in the snow?" He said, "I gotta get some pants on. It's cooooold!" Oh my gosh! This little two-year-old is a genius! He's trying to figure out what to do about those cold legs.

Some people are thinking, "Well, my kid would just stay out in the snow." Well you might have to rescue them from frostbite, but that burning sensation in his legs is a gift from God, teaching him about his decisions.

Sometimes you need to allow an experience or consequence to do the teaching; then they have something to remember about their last poor decision, rather than having a screaming or frustrated adult.

It's important to introduce freedom to your children at a young age and allow them to practice messing up while they have a safety net in their own home. You need to create a safe place for them to fail, discover who they are, and learn about life.

> Setting boundaries
> helps to create
> a safe place

What type of experience did your kids have after making a poor choice? What will they remember? What do you want them to remember?

....

....

....

....

....

....

....

....

FUN OR ROOM[1]

The phrase "fun or room" is a Love and Logic® term. It can be used to teach your child to associate their behavior with the words "no fun." "No fun for Mommy! No fun for Daddy! That thing you're doing... is no fun!"

When your children are behaving in a way that is 'no fun' for you, you can give them a choice... fun or room? They can choose to start being fun and not do the behavior that's "no fun" or they can choose their room. As a parent, you are setting up boundaries and communicating to your child what it takes to be around you. They will begin to realize there are two people to this relationship.

The challenge is to give your children a choice enabling them to feel powerful and responsible for their decisions. It's easy to take away their power and command them into obedience.

- "Fun to be with" also leads to self-control lessons for little tiny people.

- By saying "fun or room?" you are offering your child two choices, which causes your child to be powerful.

- If they don't choose either or they don't believe you are powerful, you can offer them two more choices, "You decide or I'll decide."

- If they don't choose either or still don't believe you are powerful, you can begin to move towards your child and offer them two more choices, "Feet touching the ground or feet not touching the ground?"

- If they are still not moving, then you might need to help them by carrying them to their room.

- If you find them right back in your presence and not staying in their room, which of course will happen, you can start with the first choice again... fun or room?

"My son, Taylor, is our youngest. He has been parented this way since birth. Once, when he was about two years old, he was trying to pull his sippy cup through the bottom of the top rack of the dishwasher. He began throwing a fit. I said 'Hey, hey! No fun! Fun or room?' He smiled at me and said, 'Fun!' In about one second he chose fun. You see; children are amazing. They posses self-control and powers to think and problem solve that we all too often do not expect them to exercise, and so they don't. Give them a chance and I'm sure they will impress you."

---

[1] Love and Logic ®

"Put yourself in your room if you are being no fun!"

~ Sheri

Do you see any of these challenge points in your child's life? How can you help them deal with them?

How do you affirm your children into being the individual God created them to be?

....

....

....

....

....

....

"Fun or room is my favorite tool with our two year old. I don't have a high tolerance for whining or being mean to me.
I love that I have a something that is so effective and yet so simple."

~ Brittney

POWERFUL PARENTS/POWERFUL PRESCHOOLERS

Key Ingredients to Successful Parenting

- Connection: Heart-to-Heart

- Empowerment: "What are you going to do?"

- Safe Place: "I can handle your mistakes."

- Unconditional Love: "Nothing can separate you from my love."

Powerful Parents:

- Create a safe place for their children to practice managing their choices.

- Empower their children as family members so they know how powerful they are in their relationships.

- Teach their children the importance of their connection.

> The challenge for parents is allowing their preschoolers to learn what it means to manage themsleves.

- Show their children through experience that they, as parents, are going to be protecting their child's heart.

- Sow seeds of protecting their children's heart, expecting a harvest that they will protect your heart as well.

- Learn what each other needs.

- Manage themselves while their children learn about themselves.

Steps to creating a powerful preschooler:

- Give them choices

- Let them think and problem solve

- Allow them to fail in front of you

Powerful preschoolers need to know:

- I can handle who you are

- I can handle your poor choices

- I can handle your failings

- I can handle that you're on a learning journey

- I'm going to honor you

> Children are going to teach you your capacity to love.

- I'm going to be mindful of your need for freedom as a human being in your relationship with me.

Do you feel powerful in your relationship with your preschooler? Explain.

How are you at offering choices? Can you think of more ways you can incorporate choices? For example: grocery shopping, getting dressed, meal times, helping with everyday chores, etc.

What are some areas in your child's life where you can allow them to take more responsibility and make more mistakes in a safe place you have created ... where the consequences aren't too expensive?

....

....

....

....

....

....

....

....

"Some of you are in the thick of this. You are going to make it through!"

~Danny

QUESTIONS AND ANSWERS FOR PRESCHOOLERS

These questions were submitted from our audience during the filming of this series.

Q: How can I incorporate concepts of hassle time to children three to five years old and have them actually grasp the concept?

A: *Hassle time is a Love and Logic® tool that is used when you as the parent are feeling*

hassled. The child has to pay you back for the time you felt hassled. If you felt hassled for three minutes, they have to pay you back for three minutes. They have to sit in a chair, can't get up or make any noise for three minutes. If they do, then the time starts over.

One time we felt hassled by Delani for a long time so she had to sit in the chair for half an hour; she did it because she knew how the system worked.

- Hassle time is about your child trading you time.

- They are going to experience what you are experiencing when they are hassling you.

- The purpose is to give them an option when you are at the grocery store, in the car, at church etc. You can say, "Are you sure you want to hassle me right now?

- They have a file in their head and they can ask themselves what happened the last time they hassled you.

- This isn't a threat you're not going to follow through on like… "Sit still or I'm going to smack you." Or "I'm going to pull this car over in just a minute and I'm going to smack you." When you get home follow through on the consequence.

- When your children are older, you can use this to trade chores with them. If they are not doing their chore, you can give them a harder one. You can say, "I'm feeling hassled right now, so I'm going to trade you chores."

"One thing I always tell my friends or parents that ask me advice is to make sure your children believe you. If you say, 'I'm feeling hassled' or 'fun or room,' and you never follow through, your child is going to call your bluff. So make sure that when you say something, you mean it!"

~ Brittney

Q: Can you spank a toddler?

A: *Yes, spanking is not something that is excluded from this process, but it is a very small part of it. If you are spanking your child all the time, it's a clue it's not working. Spanking is reserved for when your child is out of control and having a meltdown. Spanking is only to intervene to help your children get control of themselves again.*

Example:

Parent: *A or B?*

Child: *Waaaahhh!*

Parent: *A or B? You decide or I'll decide.*

Child: *Waaaahhhh!*

Parent: *Do you want to control yourself or do you want my help?*

Child: *Waaaaahhh!*

Parent: *No Problem. (Whack!) Is that enough or do you need another one? (Spanking is simply a whack!)*

Child: *(whimpering) That's enough.*

Parent: *Ok, let me just hold you and then we are going to go back to A or B?*

- The choice before the spanking is, "Are you going to control yourself or do you need my help?"

- When you introduce Whack! You're going to then ask them, "Is that enough or do you need another one?" They are still powerful. They have a choice.

- It's not when you as a parent have had enough and Whack! Whack Whack!

- Fun or room can be used as an option when you're at home.

- The only reason to ever use a spanking is to help your child get back to where they can decide again.

- If I allow meltdowns to happen, they become a way of manipulating every situation.

> **The point of ever introducing a spanking is to help your child gain self control again.**

Discuss these questions together as a class or in small groups.

1. What are some common areas of struggle with your preschooler? Discuss with your group some ideas you learned from this session that might help with these areas.

2. On a scale of 1-10, rate how much freedom you think you give your child? Come up with some ways you can allow them to have more freedom through choices.

3. What are some areas where more boundaries need to be established? How are you going to communicate that to your child?

4. Can you see areas where your child is teaching you self-control? In the past, how have you done in responding in love and working to protect your connection with your child?

Take some time this week to answer the questions below and apply the concepts you've learned in this session.

1. How do you show your preschoolers that you have boundaries? What are some of the boundaries that you have established for yourself? Your child?

2. Discuss your response to hearing the story of Delani and the toilet paper. What did you think of it? Learn from it? Feel about this way of parenting?

3. What type of experience do your kids have after making a poor choice? What will they remember? What do you want them to remember?

4. Go through this session and write down the answers to the REFLECT questions in your workbook.

Loving Our Elementary Kids On Purpose

session
seven

LOVING OUR ELEMENTARY KIDS ON PURPOSE
Shaping the Lives of World Changers

This session is about loving our elementary kids on purpose. It is specifically geared toward parents of elementary kids, but some of the concepts and examples can be adapted to all ages.

SESSION TOPICS

Tired or Need Something to Do?

Elementary Examples

Primary Skills to Master with Elementary Kids

Powerful Parents/Powerful Elementary Kids

Key Ingredients to Successful Parenting

Q and A for Elementary Kids

TIRED OR NEED SOMETHING TO DO?

When Delani was five years old, and in kindergarten, it was bedtime. This is often my time with Brittney to hang out and spend time together. This one night, Delani decided that she wanted to be up. She said, "Can I have a drink of water? Can I get something to eat? Can I…?" She thought of every excuse she could find not to be in bed and be with us. So pretty soon we jumped in by asking Delani, "Are you tired or not tired?" Which is also another way of saying, "Are you tired or do you need something to do?" That is what it means for her. So our girl says, "I want something to do because I am not tired." "No problem. I have plenty to do." I think it was during the winter so it was colder in the garage than in the house, which means this is a great learning opportunity for her. Before we sent her in, we asked, "Do you want to wear a jacket or just your pajamas? Do you want to wear your boots, or just bare feet?" We sent her into the garage with a broom to learn a lesson. "Clean up this mess in the garage and as soon as it's done, let me know. If you are not tired yet, I have more you can do."

She sweeps up, comes in and says, "I'm done. I'm not tired." This happened to be the month or week that we didn't get to the laundry yet. We were going to get there, it was coming, but we just weren't there yet. We had a laundry room full of dirty clothes. So I went in there and said, "Delani, can you separate the lights and the darks? She spent the next 20 minutes in there separating the lights and the darks and we were still watching a movie and hanging out. After a while, she came back with, "I'm done. I'm not tired." Lucky for us we had more laundry in the bathroom. "Alright. Come here. Same thing… separate the lights and darks…the whole thing. If you are not tired, when you are done come and find me." So about half an hour or 40 minutes went by and now we were thinking, "It is quiet. Something is different. Something has changed." We walked into the bathroom and there she was asleep on top of the pile of clothes.

She has never forgotten about this. Ever! The next time someone says tired or not tired, she reaches into her mental file and remembers the laundry and thinks, "I'm tired!"

What was your initial reaction to the story about Ben and Delani at bedtime?

How would this work with your kids?

Notice the relationship between Ben and Delani. Did they remain connected? Did he have to raise his voice or enter into a power struggle to get her to go to bed?

What do you believe is the overall goal?

....

....

....

....

....

ELEMENTARY EXAMPLES

Did You Feed The Dog?

I remember one time when I was teaching parenting skills at an elementary school. There was this mother who came up to me and said, "After learning some of these skills, I took them home with me and tried them the next day. I have been in this wrestling match with my nine year old in trying to get the dog fed. Over and over what ends up happening, "Did you feed the dog?" He says, "Yes." Then I feel lied to because he didn't feed the dog. I would check the bowl the next day and say, "When are you going to feed the dog?" Feeding the dog still ended up being my job instead of my son's job.

I listened to you and went home and said, "Alvin, do you want to feed the dog by 3pm or 4pm today?' He says, 4pm." "Do you want to come and find me, and tell me or leave a note?" "Leave a note." Because he's not going to do either, right. She says, "Great, as soon as I have a note I will know that you did." Well, 4pm goes by and there is no note saying… I fed the dog. Everybody came to dinner and he comes in and sits at the end of his table and notices that there is something different. He says, "Where is my plate?" She says, "Oh honey, hey, everyone at this table gets one meal every night and tonight I gave yours to the dog. Let me know if you want me to feed the dog for you tomorrow night." The next day he came in at 2pm and tells her, "Hey mom, I fed the dog!" He continued for weeks after on a regular routine.

Why? Because he is a genius. Yes, a genius. You see a lot folks think, "Oh no, my kid cannot go without dinner every night." That is not what happens. You don't have to do this more than one time. Kids are geniuses and will catch on. Write it down or you will forget them. You will forget to pass it on to the grandchildren.

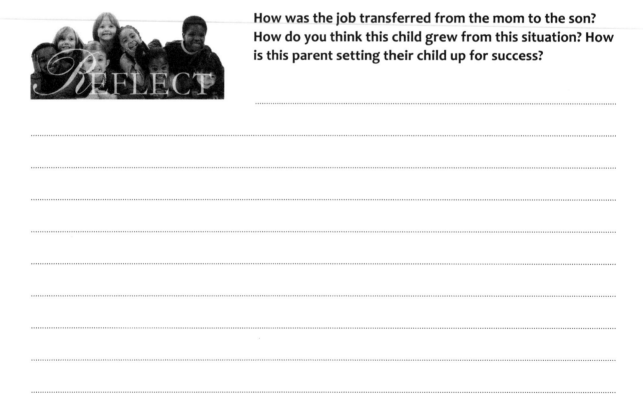

How was the job transferred from the mom to the son? How do you think this child grew from this situation? How is this parent setting their child up for success?

Oh No, Taylor is Crying Again...

I remember one time when Levi was 11 years old and Taylor was about nine years old. The routine was that the boys would fight and then Taylor would end up crying. I realized this was not just about the boys being too rough with each other; Levi was trained not to hurt his brother.

So, I started off by saying...

Danny: Levi, hey. Is your brother crying because you hurt him again?

Levi: He started it. He did it.

Danny: Yes, I bet. Hey, come over here. Have a seat. What are you going to do?

Levi: Say sorry?

Danny: Okay, all right. Taylor, come over here. Your brother wants to say something to you.

Levi: Sorry.

Danny: What do you think Tay? Do you think he is sorry?

Taylor: NO! I just think he wants out of trouble.

Danny: Oh, ok. All right, thank you buddy. Dang Levi. That didn't work well. What else can you try?

Levi: I don't know. I am going to be in this chair forever!

Danny: Maybe. Honey, what do you think the problem is? Why are you hurting your brother all the time?

Levi: I was mad at him. I'm mad at him all the time.

Danny: What happened?

Levi: He won't let me play with his friends. Every time his friends come over, he runs away and won't let me play. They talk mean to me. I can't be a part of their friends and I hate it!

Danny: Do you have some unforgiveness in your heart towards your brother?

Levi: Yes.

Danny: All right. What do you want to do about that?

Levi: I don't know!

Danny: Well, is being angry with your brother all the time and being bitter working out pretty good for you or not pretty good?

Levi: Not pretty good.

Danny: Do you want to do something about that and get rid of it or hang on to it?

Levi: I want to get rid of it.

Danny: How do you get rid of that?

Levi: I don't know.

Danny: Should you forgive him or you just hang on to it?

Levi: Forgive him.

Danny: Do you want to do that by yourself or do you want help?

Levi: I want your help.

Danny: Do you want to pray out loud or do you want me to lead you in prayer?

Levi: You can lead me.

So, I lead him through… I forgive my brother. I am not his punisher.

Danny: How do you think the Lord's heart is feeling right now? Is he pretty happy or pretty sad about this thing going on with your brother?

Levi: Pretty sad.

Danny: Do you need to clean up your mess with the Lord too?

Levi: Yes.

Danny: Do you want to do that by yourself or do you want my help?

Levi: I want your help.

Danny: Do you want to pray out loud or do you want me to lead you in a prayer?

Levi: I want you to lead me again.

So, I lead him through the prayer.

Danny: How do you feel now?

Levi: I feel better.

Danny: So, what are you going to do?

Levi: I need to talk to Taylor again

Danny: Do you think he is gong to believe you?

Levi: I hope so.

Taylor is outside playing.

Danny: Hey, Taylor. Come here. Your brother wants to say something to you.

Levi: Taylor, I'm sorry that I hurt you. I have been really mad at you for a long time. I forgive you though and don't know if you forgive me.

Taylor is just looking at him.

Taylor: Yes.

Danny: Dude, that seemed to work this time. How do you feel?

Levi: Better.

Danny: So, what are you going to do now?

Levi: I don't know.

Danny: Do you want to play or sit in the chair some more?

Levi: Go play,

Danny: See you.

How do you think Danny asking his son questions helped get to the root issue? What is the parent's role? What do you think Levi learned from this situation?

....

....

....

....

....

....

"Teaching your children to love their siblings is really important. Teach them at a young age how they can affect someone by their words or actions, especially with their brother or sister. These are great learning lessons on how to work through a problem or even to communicate how different things make them feel. I've seen many parents just adjust to the idea that 'well they just know how to push each others buttons and that's just what brothers/sisters do' instead of teaching them to communicate effectively. I remember telling my brothers that I felt hassled by them and they owed me hassle time.

Help your kids learn these tools too. Don't just keep them to your self. Give them opportunities to feel powerful with their siblings and even their friends!"

~ Brittney

PRIMARY SKILLS TO MASTER WITH ELEMENTARY KIDS

Ask great questions

Have an arsenal of choices

Do not argue ... Ever!

Hold your child accountable

Clean up messes

Prioritize your connection

- Focus on asking a lot of great questions.

- Emphasize the relational impact of the child's behavior and how it is affecting the world around them.

- Teach your children how to protect family relationships and the priority of these connections.

- Help them to take responsibility at a relational level rather than just addressing the behavior.

Say you have a dog that goes poop in the house. So you take the dog. You smack the dog. You throw it out in the yard and leave the poop there in the house. How ridiculous would that be? That's how we correct our children for their behavior. Many times, we get angry, but we leave the mess. The mess is what's happened to the relationships around them when they acted that way in our house and in our family.

- We need to teach our children how to clean up their messes.

- There are relational consequences that happen when they lie, are abusive or irresponsible. Trust is broken. Feelings are hurt.

- Emphasize the priority of the heart-to-heart connection.

  How do you think your brother feels when you act like that?
  How do you think it feels to be lied to again?

Lying isn't so much a moral issue as much as it is a relational issue

- It's not about inflicting pain to control them from the outside; it's adjusting that thing on the inside that is motivating them to lie, or cheat or hurt others.

- Teach them how to fix the broken relationship.

- Make sure they feel powerful by offering them choices: What are you going to do?

- Allow them to clean up their mess and help them when they don't know how.

- Create a safe place for them to figure this out.

How has your child's behavior affected the relationships around them?

How much of an understanding do you think your child has on how their actions affect your heart? What are some ways you can show them?

Have your children made messes that you haven't addressed?

Have you had to deal with your child lying? What can you do in light of this session

....

....

....

....

....

....

....

....

"As each child is different from one another, so is each parent.
Leave room to be yourself in your relationship with your child…
not having to do everything just like your spouse.
Keep the main things intact, but allow for individualization in relationship."

~Sheri

QUESTIONS AND ANSWERS FOR ELEMENTARY KIDS
These questions were submitted from our audience during the filming of this series.

Q: How do we work with kids with special needs like autism or ADHD?

A: *A lot of what we're sharing and emphasizing is in a general range that you can expect in any child's growing up. Then there are extenuating circumstances that require other resources and expertise. We have different dynamics such as: brain chemistry, decisions that parents have made, divorce, separation, death of a parent, blended families, medicated children, children with different challenges, etc. I am always going to refer and defer them to the experts that are available in their community. If you try to handle these situations in the general sense, you are going to be frustrated.*

Every child needs to feel safe, connected and powerful. These are basic needs that every child has, but there are going to be situations when you will need to bring in the professionals. There are people that are skilled and trained to help you create structures or use different therapies to help meet the needs of children outside of this general sense.

....

....

....

....

Q: How do you handle homework?

A: *With Delani, homework looks like, "Would you like to do it now or in 10 minutes?" I give her options right off the bat. Or I'll say, "Do you want to do it with me now or do you want to do it by yourself after dinner?" I always give her lots of choices in the decision-making process. Sometimes she says, "I can't remember, I don't remember, or I can't read." It becomes a whining process and she is basically saying, "You do it". My child's homework then becomes my homework. So I say, "I would love to help you when I feel like you're working on your problem harder than I am. There is a requirement that you talk nicely to me and that you try."*

- Give lots of choices and boundaries.

- Do what you can to make them feel powerful in the decision making process of having to do homework. "Do you want to use pen or pencil? Do you want to do it in the living room or at the counter?"

- Make it as fun as you can.

Q: What do we do when the kids figure out the tools and the tools are no longer working?

A: *You want your kids to learn the tools. This isn't about manipulation. Everyone is aware of what is happening. We are taking responsibility for ourselves in relationship. We are learning about life together and how to build strong connections of love, respect and honor. I don't want anyone to think that's a secret.*

I remember Taylor, at age 17 wanting something, and he tried to argue with me.

He says "Why? I can't believe it. This is so stupid. I can't believe you think... Why?" I said "Probably so." He said, "Ahhh, this conversation is over." That's exactly right, I will never argue with you.

As soon as I say, "Probably so," he knows this discussion has ended and I am not going to enter into a power struggle. They learn that they can't control you and that you aren't trying to control them.

- If you are firing sarcastic reaction messages to your child, you are escalating the problem.

- You need to keep your love on and lower the anxiety for it to work.

- It is not a trick!

Discuss these questions together as a class or in small groups.

1. What are some ways you could empower your children to face the consequences of their decisions?

2. What creative ways did you learn from the stories shared on how to deal with an issue? Share them and discuss ways they can be applied to your own situation.

3. What are some ways that you can help teach your child the priority of heart-to-heart connection?

Take some time this week to answer the questions below and apply the concepts you've learned in this session.

1. Write down a plan on how you are going to help your child clean up their mess?

2. Take some time with your child building your heart-to-heart connection with them.

3. What problem are you currently struggling with? Make a plan for what you are going to do the next time it happens.

4. Go through this session and write down the answers to the REFLECT questions in your workbook.

session
eight

Loving Our Teens
On Purpose

session
eight

LOVING OUR TEENS ON PURPOSE
Shaping the Lives of World Changers

This session is about loving our teens on purpose. It is specifically geared toward parents of teens, but some of the concepts and examples can be adapted to all ages.

SESSION TOPICS

Introduction

Primary Skills to Master with Teens

Teen Examples

Key Ingredients to Successful Parenting

Trust/Influence of a Parent

Q and A for Teens

INTRODUCTION

Parenting teenagers can be challenging because now, more than ever, they are close to being adults. It is difficult sharing a living space with someone who is in the process of separating from you and usually does not want what you want. One of the primary developmental tasks of a teenager is to find a way to not be you. It's nothing personal, they just have to figure out who they are. The first thing they are going to compare themselves to is you and discover how different they are from you.

In this stage of life, they also have needs they are going to try and meet... needs for freedom, validation, independence, connection with the opposite gender, etc. Find a healthy way to stay connected and to protect the relationship while this is happening. You don't want to be disconnected while your teenager is trying to get these needs met.

PRIMARY SKILLS TO MASTER WITH TEENS

Emphasize the Connection

- Connection is so important, especially in this stage of life.

- Love, respect, honor and connection are what hold your family together.

- Communicate what you need.

Empower Them to Decide

- If you don't share control it will be ripped out of your hands.

- If you don't know how to empower them, they will overpower you.

- They need power, trust and to be able to decide about their lives.

Build Gratitude

- Cultivate thankfulness.

- Being grateful is a big deal; set them up to say "thank you."

- Help them understand that there is strength from your life that is pouring into their life and it will help them and make their life more successful.

Invite Them to Think

- You want them to think and not to do the thinking for them.

- This is a great time for you to let them know what you are thinking, what works for you, and how you are seeing a situation.

> **Trying to tell your teenager what to think is a fast track into an argument.**

- Invite them to tell you what they are thinking, but be prepared. If they start telling you what they are thinking and you start bull-dozing everything that scares you, they will stop telling you what they think.

- Ask: What do you think about that? How would that work out for you?

Manage permission, opportunities & your resources

- You do not control your teenager, but you do control your permission, opportunities, and resources... the things you pay for.

"Controlling the right thing pays off for you; controlling the wrong thing is a disaster. You don't control what they think, what they value, or what they say."

~ Danny

Have you noticed your teenager trying to become their own person? How can you help and encourage them in this process?

Do they feel connected in their relationship with you? Powerful? Heard? Understood?

Are love, respect, honor and connection evident in your family? How could this increase?

How are you at managing your own resources?

....

....

....

....

....

TEEN EXAMPLES

Where Are You Going Looking Like That?

I have had the privilege of teaching parenting skills at local high schools. One of my favorite stories was from a lady who said her 14 year old daughter asked her if they could go to the mall together." She was kind of blossoming and getting some curves and bumps. She came out of her room with these tiny little shorts and a little half shirt. Everything was on display and she walked down the hall into the living room. Her mom was thinking, "Okay. I got this. I got it." All right. So mom went to her room. She pulled out the bottom drawer, reached in the back, and found some shorts, because mom has blossomed over the years too. So mom got into her little shorts and mom had a lot more going than her daughter. Mom had her tiny little shirt and shorts on and came down the hallway. The daughter looked at her mom and said, "Where do you think you are going dressed like that?" Mom said, "I am going to the mall with you. The daughter said, "I am not going anywhere out of this house with you looking like that!" Mom looked at her and the daughter goes, "Hmmf!" Her daughter went back to her room and changed her clothes.

The reason I love that story so much is that there is so much trust that this mom has for her daughter's ability to think. The mom just knows that if she shows her daughter what the mom is looking at, the daughter will come to the same conclusions and make adjustments.

> It takes an enormous amount of faith and belief in your kids to let them think and problem solve.

What do you think of this story? How did the mom turn this around?

What are some common areas of struggle for your teenager?

What are some creative ways you could get a point across to help them think and problem solve?

....

....

....

....

....

"In working with teens in ministry, I see a lot of people, including myself, get stuck when their 'Big Red Button' gets pushed. If we can identify what our button is, and unplug it, it will solve so many issues we experience."

~ Ben

Levi's Drug Talk

One time I picked up Levi from high school when he was a sophomore. He gets in the truck and we are driving down the road and he says, "I hate Mondays. Every Monday all my friends come back and all they talk about is what they did over the weekend. They got drunk. They got stoned. They got laid. That is the conversation I hear all around me every Monday.

Now inside I am thinking, "Aaaaahhh!" but on the outside I said, "Wow, bummer. What are you going to do with that?" He says, "I feel like going to a party, getting drunk and getting stoned. I don't know if I'd get laid or not, but I just want to see what this is all about." On the inside, "Aaaaahhh!" But on the outside, "Huh. How would that work out for you?" He says, "Not very good. It would really hurt you and mom, Brittney and Taylor and it would just mess everything up." On the inside, I am doing the happy dance, but on the outside, "Huh, so what are you going to do?" He says, "I need to get some new friends. I need to surround myself with some people who do something else on the weekend." On the inside, "Awwww," but on the outside, I said, "Huh, so how would that work out for you? He said, "Way better." I said, "I think you are right."

I had a couple of opportunities to blow, because my amigdyla was juiced up and I thought about control. Levi was sharing some struggles he was having in his world and I needed him to think and to consider the consequences to measure whether it was something he still wanted to do.

- It takes a whole lot of belief and momentum to trust this person with that power.

- People who are connected consider the effect of their decision on the people they are connected to. People who live disconnected don't care.

- When there is no connection, all I am thinking about is me, because I don't believe anybody else cares about me.

How was Levi able to share his thoughts and struggles with his dad?

What skills were used to help lead Levi to his own solution?

In your relationship, would your teen consider making decisions based on your connection and how it affects you and other family members?

....

....

....

....

....

Taylor's Night Away

One time, when Taylor was 16, he decided for whatever reason, he wasn't going to come home. He was 16 years old and he had his driver's license. He had all this freedom… to be home by midnight. Well, this particular night I was sick. I was up all night not having any fun. I was on the couch and woke up about 1:30. I didn't hear Taylor come home and went to his room to check and he had not come home. I texted him, "It is passed 12. Where are you?" I heard nothing. I just layed there and waited for his response and fell back asleep. I woke up at about 4 am. Still nothing. Texted him again, "If you are alive, should I call the police or start calling all your friends houses?"

Now I was really sick and still not having any fun. I fell asleep in the bathroom and then eventually moved back to the couch. Sheri got up around 6:30 am. She said, "It looks like you are not having fun." "I don't think Taylor came home last night. Will you go and check?" So Sheri went and checked. He was not there. She looked for his car; it wasn't there. Sheri began to call his friend's houses on Saturday morning at 6:30. It's not too long before all of Taylor's friends were now awake looking for Taylor and nobody could find him. About 8 o'clock in the morning, Taylor walked in through our back door and says, "My phone was dead. I slept at my cousin's house." I said, "Oh, I'm glad you are alive. Give me your keys and your phone." He acted like I just cut his heart out… because I did. I had his heart in my hand. I had his whole world in my hand. I felt so powerful now. I said, "We'll talk later."

So he went to bed. He got up at 11 o'clock. He was walking around like he was in prison. This is not the kid I want to talk to. It is about 1 o'clock or so in the afternoon and our phone rang. I said, "Taylor, it's one of your friends." Taylor came in. "Oh, that's tonight! Oh my gosh! Oh yea, okay." His friend just reminded him that there was a Halo video game tournament that night. They had matching shirts because they are a team and there are a hundred of their friends going. Taylor had just been raised from the dead! "Hi Mom! Hi Dad! How are you guys doing?" He was coming through the house, hugging people. "Hey Dad! Can I talk to you? Can we talk?"

This was the kid I wanted to talk to right there. This was the one who I wanted to be having a conversation with. I said, "I'd love to son." "I'm sorry. I should have come home last night. I should have called you. I should have told you. I'm sorry." I said, "All right. Sorry for what?" "Well, for not coming home." "Why is that a problem?" "Because you and mom were probably worried. You probably didn't know where I was." "We didn't know. We were very worried." I said, "Why is that a problem?" "I don't know. I mean because you don't want to worry." "So what's the problem here Tay? What is going on?" "What do you mean? I don't understand what you are saying." This kid grew up in our house. We had done this before. "I don't understand. What do you mean?" He was crying by now. He was really upset. "I feel like you just have somebody in your office and you are talking to me because you are my pastor or something." "Are you afraid that you are not going to get to go tonight?" "I know I'm not going to get to go tonight." I said, "Oh. I can see you are pretty scared and pretty upset, but I just want to know what you think the problem is that led to this?" "I don't know why are you asking so many questions."

Somewhere in there I get another call. I said, "I have to take this phone call Taylor. We can talk as soon as I'm done." So I left and took the phone call and he went in his room and Levi is there. He says, "Dad is doing that thing." Levi said, "Taylor, clean up your mess. You know what to do. Come on." I got done with my phone call and I don't go looking for him. I was just sitting on the couch and he came up. "Can we talk?" "Sure!" "Dad, I don't know what the problem is. I don't know what led up to this. I don't know what you are trying to get me to say." "I'm not trying to get you to say anything Tay, but can I tell you how I am experiencing being treated like this? Well, somehow your priority for your mom and me has been moved way down and I feel like we are considered least in your life. You have all these other considerations, all these other relationships that you are taking good care of, and your mom and me are way down here to the point that you don't even let me know where you are. I got stuck with the fear of maybe you are dead or hurt and I can't get to you. I got stuck with that because of your low consideration and your low value for your mom and me. That is how I am feeling." He says, "You think that?" I said, "That's how it feels. That's how being treated like this feels." "I had no idea you thought that." "That is how I'm feeling." "I'm sorry. You and mom are the most important people in my life. I don't want you ever to feel like that, I'm sorry. That will never happen again." I said, "Well, all right. That is what I needed Tay. Thank you. Do you want your keys and your phone back?" "Huh, yeah!"

Why did Taylor get his keys and phone back? What was needed?

When did Danny realize it was a good time to talk to Taylor?

What was the main point of this story? What did you take out of it that you can use?

....

....

....

....

....

....

KEY INGREDIENTS TO SUCCESSFUL PARENTING

1. **CONNECTION:** Heart-to-Heart

2. **EMPOWERMENT:** "What are you going to do?"

3. **SAFE PLACE:** "I can handle your mistakes."

4. **UNCONDITIONAL LOVE:** "Nothing can separate you from my love."

TRUST/INFLUENCE OF A PARENT

- It is my job as a parent to create a safe place for my teenager to fail.

- I need to make sure that my love stays on even though I feel hurt, scared and invalidated.

- As a parent, you are already vulnerable to your children, and to pretend that you aren't, is an illusion.

- The sooner you acknowledge that you are vulnerable to your children, the sooner you are going to see the real value they have for you.

- There is no guarantee how they will treat you. All you can do is emphasize the right things and try to set your whole family up for success.

"After a long day of challenges, laugh out loud and long!"

~Sheri

QUESTIONS AND ANSWERS FOR TEENS

These questions were submitted from our audience during the filming of this series.

Q: How can I create a heart connection when there is a disconnect present?

A: *Go back to love languages and the heart-to-heart connections session. You want to make sure that "I love you very much" messages are coming out. Change the goal from distance to connection and use these love messages to reduce the anxiety while sorting out the problems. When anxiety drops in the relationship, the dynamics change. Clean up your mess and let them know what's going on with you.*

Q: How do I start implementing these tools? Do I tell the kids or not?

A: *Whatever you feel like you need to do. Danny started implementing some of the new tools he was picking up. As for me (Sheri), I needed to say, "I am going to change some things I have been doing and do some things differently," but I needed to change over time. Do what works for you.*

> *"Get the grandparents to use the same tools you are learning."*
>
> ~Sheri

Q: What is the appropriate age to start dating and what are your thoughts about dating?

A: *Different kids can handle different levels of freedom. I have to feel like a genius to say yes to your proposal or idea. Bottom line. Put the ownership on them. You want them to be managing their responsibility and their freedom.*

Example

Parent: *You know, she is a pretty girl. I really like her. So, yes, you can date her as soon as I feel like a genius, but right now I am scared. I am scared you would not be able handle the opportunities that being alone with a girl would present.*

Teenager: *Was that a no?*

Parent: *That was a yes. Yes you can as soon as I feel like a genius.*

Teenager: *So if I make you feel like a genius, I can date her?*

Parent: *Yes.*

Every parent has different requirements. That's why your kids will say, "Well the other kids parents let them." That is because they have other things going on, but you are the parent of this child. You have to live with the consequences of your permission. You control your permission. You have to feel like a genius.

Q: What do you do with rebellion?

A: *Rebellion is classically a broken connection. You need that back before you can have any hope of them changing their behavior to protect your heart. So many parents have an adversarial relationship with their children because they don't understand that they have sown years of disrespect seeds into the relationship by "yellow-trucking" them. They think it's normal that they have the permission to treat their children like they are not human. Like saying, "I get to do their thinking, their problem solving, control their brain and get to set the rules. I have all the control and they have no control."*

- Rebellion is classically a busted relationship and they refuse to let you govern them.

- Clean up your mess, invest in the connection, be vulnerable and watch what happens.

- With out-of-control children, you may have to set limits. You can only govern the sphere of authority in your house.

- When your kid lives out there, you may need to recruit the authority that can govern out there. It is one of the kindest things you can do for your kids.

- Do you want to control yourself or do you want my help?

Discuss these questions together as a class or in small groups.

1. Would you say you are vulnerable with your teens and actually show them your heart or not? Explain.

2. What are some ways that you can show your child that you are moved by your heart to heart connection?

3. Do you have a strong enough connection with your teenager that you think they would come to you to talk about issues such as drugs, sex or other peer pressure issues? If you have talked with them about these issues, how did that go?

Take some time this week to answer the questions below and apply the concepts you've learned in this session.

1. Take some time this week and do something with your teenager to get to know more about them and what they are thinking and feeling. Write out what you learned.

2. Knowing the areas of struggle for teens, take time and share from your life experiences this week.

3. Do your teenagers know they have a safe place to fail? How are you creating this for them?

Questions & Answers

session
nine

QUESTIONS & ANSWERS
With Danny, Sheri, Britt, & Ben

These questions were asked from our audience during the filming of this series.

QUESTION TOPICS

Choices Understood

Family Reconciliation

This New Way of Parenting

Control and Choices

Time Pressures/Constraints

Physical Restraint

Sibling Rivalry

Question 1: How do you prepare your kids for situations in life where they don't really have choices... like when their teacher wants them to do certain things or their bosses when they go to work and situations like that?

DANNY: They do have a choice. They have a choice when someone barks out an order. I want my child to understand that when they respond to a person of authority who is less gracious than a parent, they still have a choice. They don't just have to take a command. Every situation is not a choice. Choices are only being offered when you are feeling resistance or a power struggle. They are experiencing commands. A situation with teachers is probably the most common.

BEN: One example I have of this came while working at a local lumberyard. The most common form of communication was screaming and yelling whenever things went wrong. One guy in particular (we'll call him Joe) would scream and get angry with me every time I made a mistake. After a few months of this, I went to Danny to get some help on what to do. So the next time "Joe" yelled at me, I was armed with advice from Danny. I looked at him and calmly said, "I would love to talk to you as soon as you stop yelling because my ears shut down when you start yelling." I repeated this a few times and it only took a day to change the way he was communicating with me. Within a week, things changed so drastically that he would say things like, "I want Ben in my workspace because he keeps me calm." Me setting a clear boundary helped him realize what I needed which in turn made our connection stronger. We have a choice in every relationship.

....

....

....

Question 2: What are the keys and strategies, as a son, to reconcile with your family?

DANNY: I think this goes back to keeping your love on. After 44 years of basically my father abandoning my brother and my family, there is plenty of time to build a case to have distance. This person does not deserve to have a relationship with me, but I do not live like that. I do not live like that with anybody. I have the love switch on and I do everything I can to keep it on.

That is step one: I manage my love... always! So when I have a reconciliation situation come up, he could have found a judgmental, accusatory, defensive distance-seeking heart. But instead, he found a heart that is practicing keeping that love on, and keeping the goal of my relationship connection. When he wanted connection back, it was ready to go.

It is tempting to want to sort through the garbage dump and want the other person to clean up their mess. You can do that, but it is probably unnecessary because what we are really talking about is the relationship from here on. I am really going for the connection, because without the connection I want justice. In connection I think, "I want to protect this."

SHERI: Does anyone have any bills? Did anyone ever try to save money? I learned that it is very hard to invest in the future when you are trying to pay for the past. I think that a part of the family reconciliation for us now is that even though that debt really is owed, I am not going to make you pay it. I am trying to invest now in our future. I don't think you really know how to have a relationship. They don't even know what to do, so even though I have been hurt so many times by parents or whoever, I have learned that I can actually reduce my expectations of you so that I'm not mad at you all the time. If I expect that you are going to give me something that you are incapable of, I am going to get disappointed every step of the way. So I reduce what I require of you and I engage you where you are able to engage me.

DANNY: In doing so, you are setting a boundary, which means that each boundary has different levels of intimacy. With each increasing level of intimacy, there is more required from the relationship. So with people that are very close to me, I have more expectation in the relationship. But in a reconciled relationship, I don't have these requirements of you. You are able to function at a certain point and that is all that is required of you. If you want to move closer, you are going to find more of who I am and what I expect in a healthy relationship. Getting closer to me requires our relationship to get healthier and healthier.

....

....

....

....

Question 3: How do you navigate this new way of parenting as a couple? How do you walk with each other when you fail and confront each other? How do you protect the connection in our marriage while you are trying to protect your relationship with your kids?

SHERI: When Danny first brought these tools home, I didn't understand the teaching that he had. We did not have the trust with each other, so it was really rough for a while. There were times when he would say, "I will engage in this conversation when you lower your voice and talk to me." *I really loved that (haha!).* I needed help, and he was picking up tools and I was not. I really did want a healthy relationship, so I would use my determination to build connection instead of protecting me.

We need to have trust and freedom and it requires us to give each other a break. There have been times when Brittney has said, "Hey mom, you are not being fun. Whatever is going on between you and dad, you need to sort it out." I have also had my teenage kid say, "I don't know what happened at work today, but you are no fun." I would say, "Ok, I am going to my room until I am fun." Some parents might think that as being disrespectful, but actually I am teaching them to communicate with me and I love them enough to let them do it. Obviously, when you first do this, you get a little touchy and clunky, but just give each other a break.

DANNY: It helps to communicate with your spouse, "My goal with you is to stay connected. I am not trying to disconnect. Can we stay connected while we work this out? What do you need from me? Did I make a mess? Do I need to clean something up?" The goal is to keep communication open and broadcast that our goal is connection while we work through this. You are going to learn a lot of great skills in that process that you can use on your kids.

....

....

....

....

....

....

....

Question 4: How do you guard against edging into control when you have a preschooler, in particular, who often does not take the choice you give them, so you end up deciding it for them. How is that not controlling them?

If you have to hold them in the chair the whole time, then what you are doing is not working. They need to understand that when you offer two choices, they have to be real choices, not one good choice and one unrealistic choice. You are going to offer two choices that make you deliriously happy. (That is what Love and Logic® calls them.) "Would you like to hold yourself here or do you want me to hold you?" Controlling is when you say, "I will teach you a lesson. I will hold you in this chair as long as I want to." That is abusive and violating control. You want to help them get self-control. I have an adult son living at my house right now, and one of the agreements of him moving back into our house was that I would help him get control of him, in some of the arrangements that we made, so that he could reach his goal. The word control is not a word I am trying to extract from this process. I am not trying to violate this relationship ever because I am trying to protect it. Violating the relationship breaks it.

....

....

....

....

Question 5: What can we do when it comes to time pressure and there is no time for choices?

BRITTNEY: For us with Delani … she's not always fun when we have to go to school. So whatever the struggle… watching cartoons, shoes not on, or not ready to go, etc., I will give my three year old as many choices as possible:

Do you want to go to school with shoes on or shoes not on?

Do you want to have lunch at school or no lunch at school?

Do you want go to school in pajamas or clothes?

Do you want to put your shoes on now or after breakfast?

Do you want to wear your shoes or carry them?

Do you want to have your backpack on or me to hold your backpack?"

Do you want to put yourself in the car or do you want my help?

Giving lots of choices helps to avoid the power struggle, especially when we are going to be late, even in the middle of being no fun. It helps them feel relieved when a big person is not trying to control them.

DANNY: Recruit the help of the school. Give them the heads up. Like, "I am bringing Missy kicking and screaming with no shoes on. They are in the bag. She has no clothes on and they are in the bag." The teacher might say, "She can come in when she is dressed." The teacher has to feel powerful. You cannot just say, "Here." That is not going to work out. If it is an option, get an adult on the other side with authority that can set limits and help with the consequences.

SHERI: I remember one time getting dressed as a young girl. I didn't like the shirt my mom had picked out and she couldn't wrestle me in it. She had to go to work and all those things, so I ended up at my aunt's house. No television. No nothing. I was bored all day. The next day my mom said to get that shirt on and it was on right away. Sometimes I think an extreme has to happen. It creates a situation that you can point to, "Remember the other day when you didn't…?" Usually you only have to do things once and they will remember.

DANNY: Don't be afraid of consequences or try to avoid them, thinking, "Oh, that would be terrible if that happened. People would think I am terrible. She would feel so bad." No, welcome it!

....

....

....

....

Question 6: My son is three years old. What do you do when they end up in their room or in a chair and physically holding them there might end up causing harming to you or to them? He is rather spirited and strong.

DANNY: If he were going to destroy everything in his room, I would keep him somewhere else where he would be less destructive. He is only three now, but he is going to get older. If you are unable to keep him somewhere now whether he can stay in the chair or not, this is going to be rather difficult later on. You have to win this one with a three year old.

So if you have to hold him from behind, then do it. You can say, "You can sit in this chair with me holding you or not holding you." This is not a bonding fellowship moment. While they are swinging, you are holding them and not talking. You are the seatbelt holding him. The seatbelt is not talking back.

....

....

....

....

Question 7: What do you do when the children have struggles among themselves? We have three boys under age five and what we constantly hear all day, "This is my car!"

DANNY: As soon as possible, you can introduce them hassle time (Love and Logic®). They need things to help them experience the weight and consequence of the way they are treating each other. They owe you time sitting in a chair or doing a chore for you (depending on their age) for the time you felt hassled.

When they say, "That is my truck or he touched me!"
I can say, "Are you sure you want to hassle me with this?"
"No, we are good. We are good."
"Are you sure? I totally feel hassled right now."

You can also add in a little motivator, "You can have some dinner as soon as your hassle time is done." You want them to feel the weight as commonly as possible.

BRITTNEY: I started to do *fun or room* with Delani when she was 10 months old. You can use that concept with the littlest one when you can't do hassle time yet. Most people think that you cannot use that with kids under the age of two, but we started with Delani when she was 10 months. She would point to her face, make a gorilla grunt and smile. Just to encourage you that you can introduce *fun or room* even with the baby and see some of the same results with hassle time for the older ones.

DANNY: Children's receptive language develops a lot faster than their expressive language. Don't be fooled by their inability to say words. Do you want some candy? They got that. You are able to introduce it a lot earlier than you think.

Resources

Loving On Purpose
Ministry of Danny & Sheri Silk
Support materials available at www.LovingOnPurpose.com

Parenting Resources from Loving On Purpose available at:
www.LovingOnPurpose.com, www.ibethel.org, www.amazon.com

Loving Our Kids on Purpose
Book by Danny Silk (Destiny Publishing, 2008)

Loving Our Kids on Purpose
Parenting Series on DVD/CD by Danny Silk

The Chicken Coop Kid
A Silk Family Story (copyright 2010)

Shorts in the Snow
A Silk Family Story (copyright 2011)

One of Those Days
A Silk Family Story (copyright 2012)

References

The Heart of the Five Love Languages
by Gary Chapman (Northfield Publishing, 2008)

Love and Logic®
Parenting with Love and Logic by Foster Cline and Jim Fay

Support materials also available from Love and Logic® at:
www.loveandlogic.com

The following phrases originated by Love and Logic®
One-Liners:

"I know"	"Probably So"	"That could be"	"I don't know"
"Nice try"	"Oh, no"	"No Problem"	
"What are you going to do?"		"How's that going to work out for you?"	

Tools:
"Fun or Room?"   "Hassle Time"